Reaching Out for Life's Best

Reaching Out for Life's Best

25 STEPS TO POSITIVE GROWTH
IN CHRISTIAN CHARACTER

WILLIAM J. KRUTZA

CONTEMPORARY DISCUSSION SERIES

BAKER BOOK HOUSE
Grand Rapids, Michigan 49506

ISBN: 0-8010-5444-3

Printed in the United States of America

Contents

Introduction 7

Section I: ***Facing Problems Around Us***

1 Dealing with Adversity 11
2 When Affliction Comes 13
3 Remaining Uncorrupt in a Corrupt World 16
4 How to Say "Blessed Are the Persecuted" 19
5 The Realities of Poverty 22
6 How to Resist the Devil 25

Section II: ***Solving Inner Problems***

7 Dealing with Anger 31
8 Overcoming Anxiety 34
9 How to Avoid Bitterness 37
10 The Cancer of Covetousness 39
11 Overcoming Doubt 42
12 Turning Fears into Faith 46
13 Taming the Tongue 49

Section III: ***Developing a Positive Personality***

14 Always Abounding 55
15 Becoming a Caring Person 58
16 Being Forgiven and Forgiving 61
17 You Shall Be Free Indeed 63
18 Gaining Those Gentle Attributes 66
19 Being Good and Godly 69
20 Humility and How to Attain It 72
21 Practicing Justice 75
22 Can You Love Too Much? 78
23 Living a Peaceful Life 82
24 Understanding One's Gifts 85
25 Have We Become More Like Jesus? 88

Introduction

God wants every Christian to become like Jesus Christ. Paul stated this succinctly in Romans 8:29. We are to be "conformed to the likeness of his Son" (NIV). That's a big undertaking. But God's Word provides the inspiration and principles for personal Christian growth.

These studies are designed to lead to positive growth in Christian character. You can study the lessons individually, with another person, during family devotions, or for a group Bible study.

Each subject is briefly defined. Inspirational ideas are included. These are followed by an intense search of the Scriptures because it is in Scripture that we discover the fullness of life. Keep your Bible open as you answer each question.

It is suggested that, at the end of each discussion, the individual or group formulate a short paragraph summarizing the primary ideas learned. This will help in future practical applications of the truths of the session.

Section I
Facing Problems Around Us

Some problems we simply have to live with. We don't have control over them. We didn't originate them. They're not our fault. We get involved simply by being human. Most are caused by the way others live.

Nonetheless, these problems are real for us. Often they are painful. They demand responses . . . and solutions!

Facing such problems in a positive manner, whether we completely solve or eliminate those problems in the process, develops Christian character. And in the end, that's what we want to happen to us.

Section 1

Facing Problems

[illegible]

[illegible]

1
Dealing with Adversity

Opposition. Hostility. Conflict with the pursuit of one's interests. Unfavorable attitudes expressed by others.

Adversity usually doesn't include the infliction of physical harm. But there's a lot of emotional anguish. This anguish often comes through harsh words—verbal abuse, character defamation, terse comments. Often adversity includes actions which interfere with the accomplishments of one's personal goals.

Adversity also comes via unfavorable circumstances such as financial setbacks, difficult working conditions, disappointing friends, or undesirable weather conditions.

1. Psalm 10:3–6 describes the prosperous wicked person. What attitudes does such a person have toward adversity? Why would he develop such attitudes? Is there validity to his approach? At what point does this approach reveal personal strengths? personal weaknesses? How do such people react when adversity comes?

2. Ecclesiastes 7:14 gives a mature person's reactions to both prosperity and adversity. Why attribute both to God? Would we say that God makes some of life rather tough? For what purpose? What does the writer mean by the statement at the end of the verse? Would one live differently if he knew what was coming in the future? Why? How? Should one be more pessimistic or more optimistic about his future?

3. Why does adversity often seem to be originated by those who know us quite well? Why do many family relationships degenerate into adversary relationships? Shouldn't love dominate in such situations? Why doesn't it?

The beginning of Proverbs 17:17 says, "A friend loves at all times" (NIV). What happens to friendship when hostility and conflict enter the relationship? Can this be avoided? How? How can these principles be applied at home?

4. David exclaimed, "The LORD lives, who has redeemed my life out of every adversity" (II Sam. 4:9). Explain the circumstances that prompted this outburst. Was he being realistic in appraising his circumstances? Compare this with Psalm 89:39–43. What would have inspired this seeming flip-flop of attitudes? Does his first outburst establish a universal principle? Will the believer always escape adversity simply by taking refuge in God? If not, what good comes from discussing one's problems with God?

5. Is the psalmist's attitude in Psalm 94:12–15 more realistic than the attitude expressed in the other passages? God allows adversity but does not forsake His children. Adversity has at least one good by-product. The person going through such circumstances is "blessed." Describe what this means. Give personal examples. What does the psalmist say will follow such circumstances?

6. What comfort can we derive from Psalm 31:7–8? Is it sufficient to know God "hast seen my affliction" and has "taken heed of my adversities"? Why?

7. What injunction does God give in Psalm 50:15? What will this do when we come in contact with those who are hostile toward us? Relate personal experiences. What happened? Have you had any experiences in which hostility turned into friendliness?

8. What attitude ought the Christian have toward others, Christians or non-Christians, who are going through adversity? What examples and attitudes are presented by the writer of Hebrews 13:3? Should this principle be universally applied? How would one realistically apply this to Christians living under a dictator? What relationships near at hand should come under this principle?

2
When Affliction Comes

In the preceding lesson we discovered adversity usually doesn't include infliction of physical harm or the presence of physical pain. Affliction goes one step further: it includes deeper pain, pain of body as well as of mind, calamity, physical suffering, or unalleviated pain (such as pain from cancer or arthritis).

Those around us can inflict pain upon body and mind through bruisings, beatings, acts of violence and war, painful psychological pressures, or even mental torture.

Some affliction is temporary. Some is permanent. We

usually have the most difficulty with what we know is permanent because the only relief is death—an unknown which carries its own form of affliction. Hope helps to overcome all affliction, especially the temporary sort.

1. Some affliction is communitywide or nationwide—the result of group sin. Consider the plagues of Egypt (Exod. 7–11). Whose fault were these? Why were the afflictions inflicted upon the people (Exod. 7:3–5)? How did Pharaoh react at first? What was the final affliction which was unbearable (Exod. 11:1–6; 12:29)? II Kings 23:26 describes affliction as God's judgment upon the sins of His people. Does such judgment still occur? Describe specific instances. What does this example teach us about national sin or national righteousness?

2. David saw beautiful Bathsheba bathing. He sent a messenger to fetch her so he could have sexual relations with her. She became pregnant. The problem: she was already married. So David had her husband sent to the front line of a battle to make sure he'd be killed. Then David married Bathsheba (II Sam. 11). What affliction did God promise would come as the result of David's sin (II Sam. 12:10–14)? What was the immediate affliction (12:15–18)? How did David first react (12:16–19)? What brought about the sudden change in his attitude (12:20–23)? What great hope is demonstrated in verse 23? Can we trace any personal afflictions to personal sins? If so, what should be done? Will this always correct the problem? How did the psalmist react (see Ps. 119:67)?

3. Scripture illustrates several uses of affliction. The psalmist says, "Blessed is the man whom thou dost chasten, O LORD" (Ps. 94:12). Solomon declared, "For the Lord reproves him whom he loves" (Prov. 3:12). What do these verses teach about the corrective values of chastening or affliction? Should we always seek to discover a lesson from painful experiences? Explain your answer. What was Job's friend's concept of affliction (Job 5:17–18)? How would you be encouraged by his words?

4. Affliction teaches endurance. Could Psalm 129:1–2 be applied to an individual as well as to a nation? What were the results of such endurance? (Check the entire chapter.) Why did Moses choose "rather to share ill-treatment with the people of God than to enjoy the fleeting pleasures of sin" (Heb. 11:24–27)? What were his rewards for enduring affliction? How does this inspire us to endure? What comfort do we get from Romans 5:3–5?

5. Job's friend Elihu said God "gives the afflicted their right" (Job 36:6). What did he have in mind (see Job 36:5–11)? What did he suggest would be the outcome after being afflicted? What do we learn from the attitude of Job toward his affliction? In severe pain, he blamed God. How did he react toward the end of his long, painful experience?

6. What did Isaiah record was one of God's great purposes of affliction (Isa. 48:9–11)? To what does he liken affliction? What well-known process was involved? Why is "for my own sake, I do it" a sufficient reason? Revelation 7:14 gives the final reason for suffering affliction. Is it worth it? What does Paul conclude in II Corinthians 4:16–18?

7. Affliction develops character. How does Job 23:10 compare with Isaiah's statements? How does Proverbs 17:3 combine the thoughts of both Job and Isaiah? Although this seems poetic, what would be the actuality while affliction is happening? Can one consider it a privilege to have such experiences (Phil. 1:29–30)?

8. God is with us in affliction. How does God involve Himself in our afflictions (II Cor. 1:3–5)? What did Paul say afflictions accomplished in his life (1:8–10)? What effect did this have on fellow believers (1:6–7, 11; 7:6–13)? What comforting words in Isaiah 53:4–5 are fulfilled in Christ's ministry to us? From Isaiah 61:1–3, describe more aspects of Christ's ministry to the afflicted.

3
Remaining Uncorrupt in a Corrupt World

Neither Webster's dictionary nor the Bible has anything good to say about corruption. It is the essence of evil. That which is corrupt has been changed from good to bad, from righteous to unrighteous. A corrupt thing is putrid, rotten and rotting, infected or defiled. It is adulterated, and debased in character. As theologians have said of the human race—depraved. Not simply deprived, but depraved—totally unable to change by human effort to reach God's standards.

Everything a corrupt person touches will itself eventually become corrupted. Like one rotten apple in a bushel, or a small open bottle of poisonous gas penetrating the air in an entire room, the corrupt person also corrupts others around him.

What insulation does the Christian have against the world's corrupting influences? Should the Christian be insulated from corruption or simply isolated from it?

1. The first mention of humanity being corrupt comes in Genesis 6:11. What preceded this (Gen. 3:1–6, 17–19; 4:8–12)? What was the condition of mankind by this time (Gen. 6:5)? How extensive was man's corruption (Gen. 6:12)? Has this changed through the milleniums since (Ps. 14:1; Rom. 3:23)?

2. In what direction are corrupt people's lives bent (Ps. 53:1–3)? What is meant by depraved? Does the last part of verse 3 mean a nonbeliever has no power to do anything good, such as love his children? What does it mean? What does Christ mean when He said, "A sound tree cannot bear evil fruit, nor can a bad tree bear good fruit" (Matt. 7:18)? What did He say ought to be done (Matt. 12:33)?

3. Exodus 32:7 says the people of Israel corrupted themselves. How did they do this? What kind of attitude did they develop toward God (Deut. 9:13)? How did Moses react to their self-corruption (9:15–21)? What was God's attitude toward this corrupting?

4. How did Paul describe those who opposed truth (II Tim. 3:8–9)? Were the two men described easily recognizable? How? In the beginning of the chapter, Paul makes a lengthy list of those who would be classified as corrupt. Are most of these grossly corrupt? Would this be the norm among the people you know? What about others? Is it possible to be looked upon as good and yet fall far short of God's standards?

5. What warning does Paul give to believers concerning association with corrupt people (I Cor. 15:33)? Where within a person does corruption begin (II Cor. 11:3)?

6. How do we "escape from the corruption that is in the world" (II Peter 1:4)? How does God fortify the believer against corruption and corrupt people (II Peter 1:3–8)? What does Peter say awaits those who practice evil (II Peter 2:9–16)? What warning does Peter give in the same chapter to Christians who become entangled with corrupt people?

7. What has happened to the believer which contrasts him with corrupt men (Col. 1:13)? How does Paul describe the believer in II Cor. 5:16–19? How did Jesus pray for His followers whom He was leaving in the corrupt world (John 17:9–19)? Pay particular attention to verse 15. Discuss how this refers more to insulating the believer from the world's corrupting influences than isolating him from being involved in the world economically and socially.

8. One of the most familiar phrases in the Lord's Prayer is "deliver us from evil" (Matt. 6:13). How does God do this for us? What keeps the righteous person going straight (Prov. 11:5–6, 8)? What special endowment does the Lord provide, and what effect does it have in the believer's life (Prov. 2:6–14)? How sophisticated or simple a prayer need we make (Ps. 140)?

4
How to Say "Blessed Are the Persecuted"

In the Beatitudes, Christ used the word *blessed* in listing nine different states of being, nine descriptions of Christian temperament or Christian attitude.

Some translators use the word *happy*. This conveys the spirit of joy Jesus wants us to exhibit. The Beatitudes illustrate a quality of life. Happy living shouldn't be an exception. It should be the norm for the Christian.

But the promise of being blessed goes beyond happiness. Happiness is a warm, pleasant feeling in enjoyable circumstances. Blessedness embraces both welcome and unwelcome circumstances: times of ease and times of hardship, times of health and times of sickness, times of wealth and times of poverty, times of acceptance and times of rejection and even persecution.

Interestingly, although the word *bless* is used in fifty variant forms in the New Testament, it never refers to material prosperity. It always refers to an inward condition.

To be blessed is to receive God's approval on one's life. This approval comes not because we deserve it or because we are perfect, but because God loves us and is gracious to us. This approval of God creates a deep and abiding satisfaction and joy, independent of outward circumstances. Thus we can believe, even through experience, "blessed are the persecuted."

1. Christ said, "Blessed are those who are persecuted" (Matt. 5:10). For what are they persecuted? Is persecution a goal of the follower of Christ or one of the results of being His follower? Is it possible for some to deliberately seek to be persecuted by non-Christians? For what will they be persecuted? Is this what is meant by having a "persecution complex"?

2. Simply because others are unenthusiastic about your religious beliefs or even drastically disagree with you, would you be right in feeling persecuted? If someone laughs at your personal list of do's and don'ts, are you justified in feeling persecuted? Is this what Christ meant? Is it legitimate for one to classify himself as being persecuted, or is this something an impartial observer is better equipped to judge?

3. Those about whom Christ spoke were genuinely discriminated against or physically harmed. They didn't look for persecution. How did the early disciples fall into this category (Acts 4:1–22)? What was the first step in their persecution (v. 3)? Did the threats of the leaders dissuade the disciples from continuing to preach about Jesus (vv. 17–18, 21)? How did the disciples respond, first to those who arrested them and then after their release? To whom did the disciples go (v. 23)? How did they pray? How did the group respond (vv. 24–30)? What happened after they prayed?

4. Christianity has always been a threat to the lifestyles of corrupt people. Their immoral behavior and unjust uses of power are severely threatened even by peace-loving Christians. Thus they often turn to violence. What does this teach about their character? How should we react to such violence? What did Jesus teach in Matthew 5:39–41? Is this difficult to do? Why? What resources can the Christian draw upon to help him follow Christ's teaching?

5. If you are not being persecuted, does this say anything about the state of your personal spiritual life? Why, or why not? Should one deliberately walk into situations in which persecution and opposition are likely to be generated? Why, or why not? Describe some such situations. Should one avoid such entanglements as often as possible? Shouldn't one's motive to be like Jesus Christ be a governing factor? What does Paul teach in Romans 8:29? What did he say would come because of such living, even without seeking it (II Tim. 3:12)?

6. What did Jesus say about why the world hates the believer (John 15:18–20)? If you were of the world, how would the world treat you? What should you do if the world treats you as "one of the gang"?

7. Where will persecution come from? Where did Jesus' own persecution come from? His family, who misunderstood His mission. Friends, such as hometown folk in Nazareth who couldn't accept Him. Members of the religious establishment, who wanted no challenge to their authority. Governmental leaders, who didn't want any disturbances. From "the world"—the general public which didn't want anyone to make them feel guilty. How would all these same elements of society be sources of persecution today? Should one be cautious not to foster opposition by being overbearingly religious? How should one arm himself to face each segment of society?

8. Don't give up in the face of opposition. What is Christ's dynamic promise to those who are persecuted for righteousness sake? Does not acceptance by God outweigh rejection by men? What other promises can the Christian cling to in times of persecution? Name as many as possible.

5
The Realities of Poverty

What does it mean to be poor? The Department of Health, Education and Welfare (HEW) has its definition. Anyone or any family earning less than a specified income is considered to be living "below the poverty level." An affluent person who has lost his affluence would consider himself poor. A college student who has to forgo an extra hamburger would classify himself as being in need.

A visit to some Asian countries, particularly India, would produce a more shocking definition. There poverty borders on desperation. People face slow starvation and death by malnutrition. People face death by disease. Some are so physically weak they can't work. Children often go hungry for days. Their bloated stomachs testify to the great food deficiencies. This is destitution—total poverty.

Maybe some of us have had financial setbacks during recessions. Some might remember the years of the Great Depression. Others have filed for bankruptcy. We've been poor, but our poverty might be classified as being rich by many in our world.

Christ and Christianity, and the Jewish religion of the pre-Christ era, have always been concerned for the poor. The Bible, some have said, is "a poor man's book."

1. How did poverty originate? The Bible doesn't give specific causes. It simply acknowledges the existence of the poor. Would sin have had anything to do with it? How? What about the fact that some people are more aggressive or more ambitious than others? Do not the ambitious usually get to the top—some have become leaders, some followers? Some are more clever than others and thus more capable to amass wealth. Do these factors have much significance, considering the fact that so many are poor? What other factors must be considered?

2. Is Hannah's prayer in I Samuel 2:7–8 a fair assessment of how some people became poor? Is this just one person's attempt to explain the plight of those around her who were poor? Can we directly attribute to God the economic conditions of a person? Is God concerned for the poor (Pss. 69:33; 109:30–31; 113:5–8)? Since it seems inevitable that some people in society remain poor (Deut. 15:11; Matt. 26:11), should we be concerned about their economic status? Why? Are there any things we as Christians can specifically do for the poor?

3. What were some of the Old Testament laws which governed attitudes and practices toward the poor? Deuteronomy 15:7–11 gave some explicit rules. What about lending money to the poor? Were the Israelites to take any collateral for loans to the poor? What about charging interest on loans (Exod. 22:25–27; Deut. 24:10–13)? How would these laws contrast with many of the lending policies of our day? In what attitude should giving to the poor be expressed? How were the people to "open wide your hand to your brother, to the needy and to the poor, in the land" (Deut. 15:11)? What was the legal status of the poor in relationship to the rich (Lev. 19:15)? How were the people to provide food for the poor (Lev. 19:9–10; 23:22)? Would such a method work in our day? Why, or why not? What do we do to fulfill this concept? How were the Israelites to treat the poor hired servant (Deut. 24:14–15)?

4. Did the law regarding the poor change in Christ's teachings? What did He tell the rich young ruler he should do (Matt. 19:21)? What about inviting the poor in to be fed (Luke 14:13)? What did Jesus teach in Luke 18:22? Did Paul follow this teaching (Gal. 2:10)?

5. Why are the privileged promised blessing for their good dealings with the poor? What are some of these promises (Ps. 41:1)? How would you explain Proverbs 19:17? What kinds of repayment can we expect from God? What attitude does kindness to the poor produce (Prov. 14:21)? Why will the person who gives to the poor "not want" (Prov. 28:27)?

6. What promises did Jesus make concerning those who show favor to the poor? What would the rich man have gained by giving to the poor (Mark 10:17–21)?

7. Why did Jesus introduce His ministry by reading from Isaiah 61:1–2? Notice that when Luke recorded this, he specifically mentioned that Jesus came to "preach good news to the poor" (Luke 4:18). What significance was there in this statement? Why did Jesus so readily associate with the poor and needy?

8. What do poor people seem to learn about the values of possessions? Do they appreciate what they obtain more than the rich? Give examples. What contrasts are made between the poor and the rich in Proverbs 19:1 and 28:6? Is there significance to Christ's choice of the word *poor* when He proclaimed "Blessed are the poor in spirit"? Why are those who are destitute in spirit "blessed"? What special choosing has God given to the poor (James 2:5–7)?

6
How to Resist the Devil

"The devil never bothers me, so I don't bother him," says one Christian.

Another seems to be troubled by the devil all of the time. Every little adversity, she claims, is the activity of Satan. She continually quotes, "Your adversary the devil prowls around like a roaring lion, seeking some one to devour" (I Peter 5:8). It seems she can see him almost everywhere she turns.

Some place between these two positions one discovers the truth about Satan and demons. You can't attribute every unpleasantry to the devil. Some are of our own making . . . or the making of family or friends . . . or such things as the weather. Knowing what the Bible says about Satan's nature and activities is a great help in learning when, where, and how to resist him.

James 4:7 says, "Resist the devil, and he will flee from you." To resist means to withstand, strive against, oppose, or affect with distaste.

1. What names does the Bible give to the devil? Carefully study the activities associated with each name. (We'll list the more significant names. Consult a topical index of the Bible for additional names.)

Accuser of the brethren (Zech. 3:1; Rev. 12:10).

Adversary (Read Job 1:6–12; 2:1–8). What did God allow Satan to do to Job and his family? What limits did God set? Can you determine why God allowed this satanic activity? I Peter 5:8 is probably the best-known text about "your adversary the devil." What does this text mean?

Beelzebub (Matt. 12:24–28; Mark 3:22–37; Luke 11:15–20).

Deceiver (Rev. 12:9; 20:2–3, 7–8, 10). Whom does he deceive? When?

Evil one (Matt. 13:19, 38–39). Notice how Christ makes "evil one," "enemy," and "devil" synonymous. According to I John 2:13–14, what was the result of encounters with the evil one?

Father of lies (John 8:44). Describe the encounter Christ had with the Pharisees, which inspired this definition (John 8:34–47).

Prince of the power of the air (Eph. 2:1–3). What does this mean? Does it apply to a sphere outside of the earth? Does this mean a physical location?

Ruler of this world (John 12:31; 14:30; 16:11). To what extent does Satan rule? What will eventually happen to his rulership?

Tempter (Matt. 4:3). Notice that this term is used interchangeably with devil and Satan in the text. See also I Thessalonians 3:4. Is Satan our tempter as he was to Christ? Explain.

2. Look further at Satan's nature. How does he sometimes present himself (II Cor. 11:14–15)? What can he accomplish under this disguise? When did he originate (Luke 10:18)? Why were he and other angels cast out (II Peter 2:4; Jude 6)? What authority does Satan exercise over demons (Matt. 12:24)? What powers does he exercise over the unsaved (II Cor. 4:4; I John 5:19)? Does Jesus use some exceedingly strong language to describe Satan's nature in John 8:44? A person possessed by Satan, Elymas, was called an "enemy of all righteousness" (Acts 13:10). Would this be a characteristic of Satan? How do Romans 5:12 and Revelation 12 present Satan?

3. How do we resist the devil? Does James 4:7 imply that this resistance is something we do physically? What concepts do we derive from I Peter 5:8–9? Ephesians 6:12 makes it clear "we are not contending against flesh and blood." Would this eliminate the concept of physical contact? If so, what do we mean when we talk about wrestling with the devil? Is Satan ever a physical being? Does the Christian's withstanding of him involve resistance to evil personalities and concepts rather than the occurrence of physical encounters? Describe "principalities," "powers," "rulers of this present darkness," and "spiritual hosts of wickedness in the heavenly places."

4. We get a rather clear picture of who to resist. But how does one do it? First notice Paul's instruction to "take the whole armor of God" (Eph. 6:13–17). How would one "take" this? Are we to be involved in something physical? Why, or why not? Discuss each aspect of the armor. How many of the pieces seem to require no activity? How many require an exercise of faith? Where does prayer fit in? What advice does James give when he commands the Christian to resist the devil (James 4:7)? What does he say in the next verse? How does one "give no opportunity to the devil" (Eph. 4:27)? Discuss some present-day situations in which this concept can be applied.

5. Where can the Christian go for protection against the devil (I John 5:18)? How does Christ supply the needed protection to the believer (John 10:27–30)? What positive actions can the Christian engage in because of the powers of Christ within (Luke 10:17–20)?

Section II
Solving Inner Problems

Some problems are of our own making. We can't blame others, or even the devil. They come because of who we are. "Personality problems," we often call them at our house.

And all people seem to have these problems. They're part of human nature . . . which often appears to be too human. Our bent toward sin has something to do with it. Environment (for instance, our upbringing) has to be considered. Just because we have joined Jesus doesn't mean we've suddenly become angels!

Many of our problems are inner problems. Some of them don't ever surface. They're not visible, like skin rashes, although many can cause disturbances others notice. Sometimes others might wonder, "What's gotten into him?" or "What's eating him?"

These inner problems have a way of becoming perennial. But with the help of our problem-solving God, they don't have to come into full bloom. If we cultivate more of the fruits of the Spirit, we have a good chance of overcoming many of these inner problems. But, as a gardener searches out weeds, we must keep a constant vigil lest these problems take over. We need constant spiritual cultivation.

7
Dealing with Anger

None of us has to be told what anger is. We usually know it when we see it, in others or in ourselves. It's the exceptional person who can honestly say, "I never get angry." Maybe a few milquetoasts would never show outward anger. You'd never catch others in an angry act. They internalize it—they have ulcers or heart disease.

Anger has many expressions, many shades, all of them gray. To be angry, says the *Oxford Universal Dictionary*, is to be full of troubled activity, troublesome, negatively affected by situations, vexed, to feel or show resentment, smart, or become inflamed.

Add to this becoming irate—enraged, incensed. Or irritated—provoked, stirred up, aggravated, exasperated.

Add to this wrath—vehement or violent anger, intense exasperation or resentment, deep indignation, righteous indignation, or impetuous rage.

Wow! Others had better stay out of the way!

Do I have a right to become angry? Was anger one of the emotions God originally built into human personality? What does it mean that God gets angry? Is anger totally the result of sin and one of the expressions of one's sinful nature? Can anger ever be a useful emotion, expressing rage against injustices and evils in our society?

1. How do we explain the use of the word *anger* in reference to God? Many texts relate that "the anger of the Lord was kindled against . . ." (Exod. 4:14); "the anger of the Lord blazed hotly" (Num. 11:10); "the anger of the Lord was kindled against them" (Num. 12:9; 22:22; 25:3; 32:10, 13). What seemed to be the common denominator of these situations? Check additional references in Deuteronomy (2:20), Joshua (7:1; 23:6), and Judges (2:14; 3:8). Why did God seem to get upset with His own people, Israel? How many of the dictionary definitions can be used in describing the anger of God? Did God become exasperated and deeply indignant? Which definitions cannot be applied to God's anger?

2. Sin has alienated mankind from God. Man goes the opposite way from what God originally designed. He is totally unable to please a holy God. No wonder Scripture writers picture God as angered at the sinfulness of man. What do the following texts teach about God's attitude toward sin? Deuteronomy 9:20 deals with the making of the golden calf by Aaron. I Kings 11:9 depicts Solomon as a lover of women and having a lack of love to God. I Kings 18:17 shows Elijah condemning Ahab for his sin. The writer of Ecclesiastes 5:4–7 asks, "Why should God be angry at your voice"—because people make vows which they never intend to honor. Does God have a right to such anger?

3. The psalmist asks God, "Wilt thou be angry for ever?" (Ps. 79:5). He asks this again in Psalm 85:5, adding, "Wilt thou prolong thy anger to all generations?" How do we interpret these verses? Does this jibe with our views of God being merciful and forgiving? What interpretations could be placed on these psalms?

4. How do we respond to texts such as Psalms 103:8 and 145:8, which describe the Lord as merciful, slow to anger? Are these fortified by Joel 2:13, which says God "is gracious and merciful, slow to anger, and abounding in steadfast love," and Nahum 1:3, "The Lord is slow to anger, and of great might"? What do the contexts of these statements teach us about God?

5. Although it's difficult to explain how God can become angry, it's not difficult to explain human anger. What causes one to become angry? Is most anger produced when others challenge our sphere of knowledge or authority? What else produces anger? How?

6. What do the Scriptures teach about overcoming anger? How can we fulfill Ecclesiastes 7:9, "Be not quick to anger"? How does the last half of the verse prompt us to control our anger? What adverse effects does anger produce (Prov. 27:4)? Should we actively oppose getting angry? How (Ps. 37:8)? What type of character is demonstrated by one who is slow to get angry (Prov. 16:32)? Why is it so difficult to be positive and creative when one is angry? What principles does James 1:19 give? How does one's speech and anger go together?

7. Why is it so important to dispose of anger quickly? What help does Ephesians 4:26 offer? How can we act on this advice? What effects would Proverbs 15:1 have in a tense situation? How can you practice the advice in Romans 12:19 in your life? Which of the fruits of the Spirit (Gal. 5:22–23) affect one's feelings of anger? How?

8
Overcoming Anxiety

Anxious. All of us get that way at least once in awhile. But some continually worry about the future. Problems are sure to come. You dread what's coming next. You have periods of intense worry and concern. You believe some catastrophe, either personal or national, is inevitable.

Anxiety affects body as well as mind. Some have breathing difficulties, excessive perspiration, headaches, dizziness, restlessness, an inability to sleep. Some people fear new situations, or are insecure in social situations. Slight stresses cause some people great discomfort. They have feelings of inadequacy and inferiority.

People worry about job security, unemployment, higher costs of living on fixed income, higher bills, or serious illness. Some people are facing death because of an incurable disease. For others, heart disease causes inactivity. Runaway or rebellious children may worry you.

These are causes for anxiety—if we allow ourselves to worry. But the Christian is commanded, "Have no anxiety about anything" (Phil. 4:6). Is this idealistic, or can we learn to live that way?

1. What things in life produce most human anxieties? How would these be different in various parts of the world? Would we say that economics have considerable bearing on the amount of anxiety expressed by an individual? What in our natures longs for security? How secure can the average person be in his job? What threatens job security? How can one's medical condition produce anxiety? Do most of us become anxious sometimes in our lives?

2. When Jesus talked to Martha, He said, "You are anxious and troubled about many things" (Luke 10:41). List some of the things that seemed to upset Martha. How would these things affect us in our culture? Did Jesus imply that Martha's sister Mary had no anxieties? What did Mary discover as an antidote to anxiety?

3. How does Jesus' teaching in Matthew 6:25–34 mesh with our attitudes about the future? Is life as simple today as Jesus described? Does He mean we should show no concern about food or clothing? What additional elements or illustrations does Luke 12:22–31 put into the narrative? What is the difference between being concerned and being anxious? When do we cross the line from the one into the other? What essential truth did Jesus desire to teach in these passages?

4. According to Job 5:8–11, what does God provide for all mankind? What understanding did the psalmist (Ps. 104:5–30) have of the providential goodness of God? What, besides humanity, comes under the providential care of Almighty God (Ps. 145:15–16)? Do you agree with the assessment of the writer of Ecclesiastes 2:24–26 and 5:18–20?

5. Are peace and anxiety opposites? Discuss. Does "he [God] makes peace in his high heaven" (Job 25:2) have anything to do with our obtaining peace? What does this tell us about God? How do we sense that "the God of peace" is with us (Rom. 15:33)? How does this attitude rebuff Satan (Rom. 16:20)? Why does Paul contrast confusion and peace in I Corinthians 14:33? What was

Paul discussing that led to this conclusion? Name the conditions Paul says will produce the sense of God's peace being with the believer (Phil. 4:8–9). Why can one "cast all your anxieties on him" (I Peter 5:7)?

6. Jesus made it clear He would give us peace (John 14:27). How does one receive peace from Christ? What are the results? How did the psalmist express this in Psalms 29:11 and 72:7? How extensive is God's gift of peace (Isa. 57:19)? If peace is a gift, can we do anything to obtain it? Why, or why not? How does peace truly become a part of our character?

7. Notice the command Jesus gave to the winds (Mark 4:35–41). Can God, who brings peace into nature, do the same in human nature? What conditions are different?

8. We are commanded to live at peace with others. How much effort should be extended to accomplish this (Rom. 12:18; II Cor. 13:11)? How does Jesus describe those who make a special effort to become peacemakers (Matt. 5:9)? When one makes an effort at being peaceful and a peacemaker, what does this do to one's feelings of anxiety? How should one be involved in being a peacemaker in relation to international problems?

9. End the session by reading (in unison, if this is a group Bible study) Romans 15:13.

9
How to Avoid Bitterness

Bitter things are acrid, obnoxious, biting to the taste. They irritate the nerves that control taste. Quinine, wormwood, and gall are examples that most people would name. Others would add aspirin, lime peelings, beer, Epsom salts, or gourds to the list. Still others would include anything with a pungent taste.

All of these items describe things that are bitter in the mouth. But what describes bitterness in the spirit or the heart of a person?

This kind of bitterness entails an adverse frame of mind, anguish of heart, or animosity. A bitter person expresses intense grief or resentment. He feels enmity toward others—or toward God.

Bitterness doesn't sound like anything you'd stand in line to obtain. It isn't something a healthy-minded person wants to develop. Unfortunately bitterness can creep into even the best of us.

1. What factors in life produce bitterness? Does the bitter person usually blame outside circumstances and other people . . . and possibly God? Give examples. Would bitterness gradually become more intense? What are some of the factors which would intensify bitterness? Is it possible to cover up bitterness? How? What are some of the psychological effects of bitterness? How can bitterness produce physical and mental illness?

2. The words *bitter* and *bitterness* are frequently found in Scripture. Would this suggest that bitterness is an age-old problem? Of course, there are references which allude to the sense of taste, such as the reference to water which had an unpleasant taste (Exod. 15:23–25). What had happened to this water to make it bitter? How was it made drinkable? How was the use of bitter water later used as a form of punishment for an unfaithful wife (Num. 5:11–24)? Wasn't this concoction of bitter water seemingly crude and cruel (vv. 16–17)?

3. How did Job reveal his bitterness (Job 3:1–25)? He prefaced his remarks about bitterness of soul with the question "why?" Did he ever receive a satisfactory answer to this question? Explain. Read Job 23 also. Notice he begins, "Today also my complaint is bitter" (Job 23:2). Describe his complaint. What values are there in the openness of soul Job demonstrated in 7:11? How therapeutic are his utterances in 10:1–2?

4. What did the writer of Ecclesiastes find "more bitter than death" (Eccles. 7:26)? Why would this be so? Was he not being quite biased (vv. 27–28)? What was this saying about human relationships being the causes of most bitterness? How could he compare this to death, which he had not experienced?

5. Is bitterness a self-imposed malady? What about hardships imposed by others? What is the difference (Exod. 1:8–14)? How much bitterness can be traced to personal and national sins (Jer. 2:19; 4:18; Amos 8:7–10)? How does the writer describe the end of one who indulges in immorality (Prov. 5:1–4)? What provision is made to avoid the bitterness resulting from such indulgence (5:1–2)? Why does Isaiah predict woe for those who "put bitter for sweet, and sweet for bitter" (Isa. 5:18–23)?

6. What are some of the first steps to overcoming bitterness? What good is self-analysis (Prov. 14:10)? What place does weeping have in eliminating bitter attitudes (I Sam. 1:10; Isa. 22:4; Matt. 26:75)? Is it legitimate for men to weep? Explain why they usually don't.

7. How is it possible to become bitter because of the actions of those close to us? What advice does Paul give in Colossians 3:19 concerning husband-wife relations? Who should take the initiative? How can bitterness develop in such an intimate relationship? How can it be removed without damage to the relationship?

8. James asks the penetrating question: "Does a spring pour forth from the same opening fresh water and brackish?" (James 3:11). To what is he referring? What do bitter words tell about the condition of the heart? What does Ephesians 4:31 advise? How would Ephesians 4:32 remedy the problem of bitterness? How does "the grace of God" help to rid a person of any "root of bitterness" (Heb. 12:14–15)?

9. What are the opposites of bitterness? List these, along with any supporting Scriptures.

10
The Cancer of Covetousness

Keeping up with the Joneses is an American mania. Yet it is an almost total impossibility, because the Joneses always seem to be one step ahead of their rivals or neighbors. Still this passion seems to consume most of us. And when we can't duplicate what a neighbor or friend or relative has, we either attempt to find an imitation that only an expert can detect or else we buy what the Joneses have. "I wish I had a car like. . . ." "I wish we had a house like. . . ." "I wish I had a beautiful wife like. . . ." On and on . . . until one develops a burning passion to have what others have.

Coveting. That's what the Bible calls it. But what does it mean? And what effects does it have on the covetous person . . . or on the coveted?

To covet is to lust after someone, or to have a vehement desire (e.g., strong sexual passion). A covetous person often longs for a particular object, especially something that belongs to another person. To covet further means that a person eagerly desires something, or has an inordinate desire to possess something.

The Bible's clearest statement about coveting comes in the moral law given by God through Moses—the Ten Commandments. The commandment about coveting is a vital moral concept. It deals with an important issue, even though it seems that covetousness hurts no one. We ask ourselves, "How can my 'I wish' hurt others?"

1. God declares, "You shall not covet your neighbor's house; you shall not covet your neighbor's wife, or his manservant, or his maidservant, or his ox, or his ass, or anything that is your neighbor's" (Exod. 20:17). How would you rewrite this in today's terminology? What more would you include in describing "anything that is your neighbor's"? How relevant are "manservant, maidservant, ox, ass" in our sophisticated culture? Do we have any equivalents? List these.

2. Notice what this commandment includes. First, a man's most longed-for possession—a place to call his own, his home. Second, a man's most prized earthly relationship, provided by his most intimate associate, his wife. Then those people who supply his needs or fulfill his wants. Finally his means of making a living—because oxen and asses were exceedingly necessary in an agrarian culture. Why do we think God made such a clear law regarding these? Why would one seem to covet these possessions of his neighbor's so strongly? Is it because, especially in the Old Testament era, the average person had little beyond these? How strongly would all this apply today?

3. What seems to be the next step beyond covetousness? What did Achan do after he coveted (Josh. 7:18–21)? What was the punishment (7:14–15)? Was the punishment for covetousness or for its results? Is the same progression evidenced in Micah 2:2? Does this mean that if we covet something that others possess, we are dangerously close to trying to get it by means that are not legitimate? If not, do we need to worry about the sin of coveting? Why, or why not?

4. Why are the covetous listed among such horrible sinners by Paul (Rom. 1:28–32; Eph. 5:3–5)? With what other sins does he associate covetousness (I Cor. 5:10–11)? What strong condemnation does he say is coming to such people (I Cor. 6:9–10)? What is their means of salvation (I Cor. 6:11)? Paul says covetousness will be rampant in "the last days" (II Tim. 3:1–5). What is his advice concerning association with such people? (See the last phrase of verse 5.) What drastic step does the apostle suggest is necessary to rid oneself of covetousness (Col. 3:6–10)?

5. Is covetousness rampant today? How do we determine this? Has covetousness not been a perennial sin throughout history? What did Jeremiah say about the people of his day (Jer. 6:13; 8:10)? Where did Jesus say coveting originates? Could anyone blame others if he were covetous (Mark 7:20–23)? What warning did Jesus give to the person desiring that his brother divide his inheritance (Luke 12:13–15)? What did Jesus say "a man's life does not consist of"? What are the most important aspects of life? What about the development of the mind and of the soul? Do these occupy enough of our attention? What did Jesus teach ought to be our top priority (Matt. 6:33)? What does He say about the place of material things in one's life?

6. What did the psalmist ask for in contrast to getting gain—or coveting (Ps. 119:36)? Why will "he who hates unjust gain ["covetousness," KJV] prolong his days" (Prov. 28:16)?

7. Hebrews 13:5 (KJV) says, "Let your conversation be without covetousness." Why would this admonition be given? Should we ever talk out our wishes? How can we keep our wishes from developing into overt coveting of what others possess? How would a generous attitude toward others, regardless of whether they have less or more than we do, help dispel covetousness?

11
Overcoming Doubt

Some people are gullible. They believe almost everything they're told. Often they afterward discover they've been hoodwinked. They then don't know what to believe.

Others are just the opposite. They are skeptics to the *nth* degree. They won't believe anything without black-and-white proof. Then they still have reservations.

In between are the majority. They doubt some things; they are perhaps wary because of past gullibility. They continually have reservations about what to believe, but are open to believe once something has been sufficiently substantiated by credible witnesses.

Thomas, one of Jesus' disciples, was in this category. He's been called "doubting Thomas." And anyone who doubts, even today, picks up this nickname.

Consider the facts about Thomas. Maybe you'd doubt, too! He wasn't in the group when Jesus revealed Himself after His resurrection. Thomas seemed to think the other disciples were asking him to believe something earthshaking—sight unseen. The disciples told Thomas they had seen the risen Christ. Thomas responded, "Unless I see in his hands the prints of the nails, and place my fingers in the mark of the nails, and place my hand in his side, I will not believe" (John 20:25). Eight days later, Jesus appeared when Thomas was with the group. Jesus urged Thomas to touch His wounds. "Doubting Thomas" made an about-face. He really should be known as "Believing Thomas." He exclaimed, "My Lord and my God!" (John 20:26–29). A doubter can be changed into a believer.

1. Doubt is a state of mental and moral uncertainty as to the truth, validity, or reality of a given idea or substance. It is the condition of being uncertain. To doubt is to be undecided in opinion or belief, to mistrust, to call into question, or to hesitate. Give some examples of when it is wise to doubt. Can doubting become a vehicle to belief? Explain. Should everyone maintain what is called a "healthy skepticism"? Explain. Give examples. What values can such an attitude produce? Explain the difference between doubting and holding reservations about the validity of some presented facts. How can this be applied to one's Christian faith?

2. Matthew 28:17 describes two reactions to the risen Christ. What was the first reaction? By whom? What was the second reaction? Would it have been justified considering the momentous occasion? What made this situation unique? How did Jesus respond to both attitudes (Matt. 28:18–20)? Had Jesus ever encountered doubt before? How did He treat doubt in the account in Matthew 21:21? How did the doubting father in Mark 9:17–29 respond to Jesus' demand for faith? How can unbelief be overcome? Discuss Jesus' positive teaching in Mark 9:23. How would this eliminate unbelief?

3. Is anything wrong with an attitude such as that stated by Thomas in John 20:24–25? Would this be labeled "healthy skepticism"? How long was it legitimate for Thomas to be a doubter? What changed his mind?

Was not a similar doubt expressed in Acts 2:12–13 concerning the infilling of the Holy Spirit? How was this doubt expressed? How did Peter help the doubters (vv. 14–40)? How strong do proofs need to be before they are worthy of acceptance? Does anyone have a right to doubt Christian truths today? Why, or why not? What about needing proof beyond Scripture, such as that given by the testimony of Christian believers? What happened to the Israelites because of unbelief (Heb.

3:12–19; 4:6–8)? What does this text say about receiving the good news and failing to appropriate it?

4. Matthew 14:22–33 describes Christ walking on the water and Peter's spontaneous response, "Bid me come to you on the water." What caused Peter to begin sinking? In what exact words did Jesus respond to Peter's cry for rescue (v. 31)? Why would He attribute Peter's sinking to doubting? Carefully explain what Peter doubted. Was there any evidence of a change of attitude? Describe.

5. How do we define what Christ meant by "does not doubt in his heart" (Mark 11:23)? Are there different levels of doubt? What does Jesus propose in the same verse as an antidote to doubt? What great prayer principle immediately follows this verse? Why is belief so important to prayer? What injunction does Paul give in I Timothy 2:8 (see KJV) regarding doubt when one prays?

6. Belief and/or faith counteract doubt. Why? How? What great principle of faith is given by Paul in Philippians 4:13? How does this overcome doubt? Repeat what Jesus said about "all things [being] possible" in Mark 9:23. To whom does this apply? What further assurances are given in Matthew 19:26, Mark 10:27, and Luke 18:27? How are we to respond once we have prayed (Matt. 21:22)?

7. Give personal testimonies of situations in which people who were doubters later became believers. Explain the process which brought about the change. Possibly you (or others in the group) still have doubts. This would be an excellent time to express such doubts and have other Christians, in love and understanding, respond.

12
Turning Fears into Faith

Some fears seem legitimate—for example, fear of being alone or unprotected in a crime-ridden neighborhood, fear of not making it to shore in a rowboat on a large lake when a sudden windstorm develops, or fear of running out of gas when you're stranded in a snowstorm.

But many fears are not rational. They are labeled phobias. These are fears of objects or situations which, in themselves, pose no actual danger. Most phobias have rather long descriptive names: for instance, acrophobia—fear of high places (even when one is in an enclosed observation tower); astraphobia—fear of lightning and thunder; ereuthophobia—fear of blushing; gynephobia—fear of women; hematophobia—fear of blood; ochlophobia—fear of crowds; or pyrophobia—fear of fire.

People suffering from phobias will go to great extremes to avoid whatever produces the fear. The intensity of fear associated with a particular object may range from irritating concern to serious distress and even attacks of extreme anxiety.

Usually such phobias are best treated through formal counseling. One doesn't turn to simplistic answers to deep-rooted problems. An understanding of why one has these fears is basic to any corrective therapy or cure.

But many fears aren't results of such twists of thinking, although they become quite deep-rooted in the personality. Most seem to develop out of threats to one's security or prestige. These have a spiritual as well as a mental nature. They should be dealt with on the spiritual plane.

1. Webster defines the noun *fear* as the emotion of pain or uneasiness caused by a sense of impending danger or the apprehension of evil; a state of alarm or dread. The verb means to be filled with fright, apprehensiveness, or anxiety.

First, perhaps you have a phobia that you would like to discuss with others. Some of these may be amusing, but be considerate, because phobias are serious problems to many people. If someone else has had a similar phobia, ask how he or she overcame it.

Give any examples of fears you have had, such as fears of unemployment. Did you feel justified in having such fears? Are constant fears ever legitimate? Explain. How did you overcome your fears? How do you keep them from reoccurring? What do you do when they reappear?

2. What causes fears of personal or national security? What situations did the psalmist find himself in (Ps. 31:11–13)? What attitude of heart did he display? Jeremiah 6:25 and 20:10 describe rather common situations in his day. Are these still reasons for fearing? What kinds of fear do these situations produce? Is there a danger in not having such fears? Explain. How does a nation overcome such fears? Are our present answers to such fears enduring? Will these answers eventually work in eliminating the sources of our fears? If not, what approaches ought to be taken? How can we promote such concepts?

3. Can a nation depend on God to "preserve . . . from dread of the enemy" (Ps. 64:1)? How can this verse be extended to include an entire nation? Is fear an individual matter, whereas national fear becomes hysteria? How does fear of an enemy affect the policies of a nation? Give examples. How does this fear affect an individual? Did God hold fear and dread over the heads of the children of Israel if they didn't obey His word (Deut. 28:58–68)? Had the Israelites a right to be afraid if they disobeyed?

4. Why do we often have fears about personal security? Are we too geared to security in our society? Can one become phobic about security? How would Psalm 37:5–7 help in such situations? What about fearing for one's reputation?

5. What was Christ talking about in Matthew 10:26–28? Whom shouldn't we fear? Whom should we fear? Why "fear him who can destroy both soul and body in hell" (v. 28)? Who is this? How should one express this fear?

6. Is fearlessness a product of our new nature in Christ? What does Paul say in Romans 8:15? What does he imply fear does to a person? What does "the spirit of sonship" have to do with it? How did Paul repeat this idea in II Timothy 1:7? What positive elements did he state are in contrast to fear? How would these operate in one's life?

7. John proposes quite an advanced philosophy when he states, "There is no fear in love, but perfect love casts out fear" (I John 4:18). What does he say fear is associated with? How does love overcome this? Explain why there is "no fear in love." Does this have something to do with trusting and appreciating other people? Would both parties have to adhere to the principle? Why, or why not? What would constitute "perfect love"? How is this attainable?

8. How does a sense of the presence of the Lord eliminate fear? How can one practically apply, "The Lord is my shepherd. . . . I will fear no evil: for thou art with me" (Ps. 23:1, 4, KJV)? Aren't some rather strange methods used to protect the believer (Ps. 23:4–5)? How would you apply the assurances in Psalm 46:1–3 to your life?

9. What is meant by fearing God? The people of Israel were commanded: "You shall fear the LORD your God" (Deut. 6:13; see also 6:24; 8:6; 10:12, 20 for a few examples). "The fear of the Lord is the beginning of wisdom" (Ps. 111:10; see also Prov. 1:7). How can this be? Are we to be afraid of God? Why do we define fear as "reverence" when thinking of our relationship to God? Is this the best meaning? Is the prophecy of Jeremiah 32:40 something desirable? Is this type of fear the best way to eliminate fears? Explain.

13
Taming the Tongue

"If only I would have kept my mouth shut!" It's a rare individual who has never had to confess this. Somehow most of us possess the ability to say what ought not be said—or what should have been phrased in much more acceptable language.

Others exist who seem to have what could be called

"mind and mouth disease"—a fancy name for the ugly practice of gossiping. They relish getting the "lowdown" on others and then telling it to as many people as possible, often embellishing it to make it more interesting or sometimes slanderous. But gossiping is far more than a disease. Several passages in the Bible list this malady of the mouth along with covetousness, deceit, murder, insolence, faithlessness, heartlessness, or ruthlessness (Rom. 1:28–31); or with jealousy, anger, selfishness, conceit, disorder, and quarreling (II Cor. 12:20).

Unfortunately, far too many of us become gossips under the seemingly innocent guise of "I just thought you should know this about. . . ."

1. List all of the sins mentioned in Romans 1:28–31 and II Corinthians 12:20. Why would gossip be classified among such heinous sins? Are any of the other attitudes related to gossip? How? Could some of the other descriptive words be put as modifiers of gossip (for example, heartless, ruthless)? Compare others.

2. How do you define gossip? What do you mean by idle talk and tattling? Why is it so easy to gossip? Does our national preoccupation with personalities (e.g., interest in what Hollywood stars do off-screen) foster a freer attitude toward gossip? Do some people believe that gossip peddling, such as that by gossip columns in the newspapers, legitimizes the practice?

3. How would you link gossip to the concepts presented in Proverbs 11:13 about talebearers? in Proverbs 12:17 about deceit? in Proverbs 14:5 about lies? How does the psalmist describe the causes and effects of gossip (Ps. 50:19–20)? What link exists between gossiping and listening to ill-conceived ideas (Prov. 17:4)? In what class does Proverbs 10:18 place the slanderer? What specific anti-gossip command is given in Leviticus 19:16? Could this apply today? How?

4. Proverbs 6:16–19 has often been described as a listing of seven deadly sins. Which ones are related to the use of the tongue? How are they described? What effects do these have, first on the speaker and then on those about whom he speaks? Why do you think the Lord would place such a great emphasis on the sins of the tongue? How would Psalm 140:3 corroborate the intensity of the comments in Proverbs? What type of people does Psalm 64:3–4 describe? What is the condemnation listed in verses 7–8?

5. How does James 3:2–12 describe the tongue? Is it a nice picture? What does James say? Why is the picture so black? To what does James liken the tongue in verses 4 and 5? in verse 6? To what does he compare taming the tongue (vv. 7–8)? What contradictions does he say the tongue produces (vv. 9–10)? Would these be problems in the Christian's life? Why? Does James seem somewhat unable to comprehend why all this is so (vv. 11–12)? Does he offer any correctives? What? Why?

6. Where does the gossip's problem originate? What did Jesus say was the root of the problem (Matt. 15:10–20)? In I Timothy 5:13, Paul made some interesting observations about idle talk. What are these? What problem does he attribute to men who are "empty talkers" (Titus 1:10)? How are these problems corrected? If a transformation is necessary, would Christian conversion take care of the problem? Why are there many Christian gossips? Would they be under the condemnation of God? In what ways? How can they change?

7. Where does one turn for a cure? Notice first what the psalmist says about the ferocity of the tongue in the latter part of Psalm 120:2–3 before reading the first phrase of verse 2. Next read the opening plea. How is this a cure? How would this come about? What does the psalmist mean in 141:3? How does the Lord accomplish this?

8. How does Psalm 19:14 supply a corrective for gossips? How would this apply in everyday conversation? Give some examples. Would Psalms 34:1; 40:3; 71:8 put any limits upon how we talk or what we say? How? What further guard would Psalms 71:15 and 37:30 provide? Are these good for us?

9. Do we leave all this to the Lord? How are we to be involved? How did the psalmist cooperate (Ps. 39:1)? What does Zechariah 8:16 say we must do? How does this affect gossiping? How does a person keep his tongue controlled on a continuing basis?

Section III
Developing a Positive Personality

Life isn't all problems. Nor should one approach life with too great an emphasis on problem solving. If you listen to many Christian leaders today, that's all you'd get. They miss some of life's great positives!

Advancement in Christ-likeness comes more from the development of positive characteristics than from the elimination of the negatives.

Of course, that doesn't say we should overlook the negatives. And anyone who preaches this philosophy is presenting only half of the gospel. Negatives exist and must be dealt with. That's what we have been doing up to now. If you don't deal with the negatives, they often get worse and squeeze out the development of the positives or neutralize one's life so there is no search to fulfill the positives. But once negatives have been treated, we can progress in Christ's direction.

Now to some of the great positives! There are many.

And if you apply the basic principles of each one, you'll definitely discover positive growth in your Christian life. That's the purpose of this entire book.

14
Always Abounding

To abound means to overflow, to be plentiful, to be rich, or to have to overflowing.

Not one of us would turn his back on happiness. We all desire to overflow with joy, have happiness in abundance, and be rich in those things which have lasting and satisfying values.

It's all possible. And you don't have to take a possibility-thinking course to make it all happen.

You simply take a new approach to what you have received because of your relationship to God through Jesus Christ. Take stock of what you possess in Him. Consciously turn on the positive switch, because nothing from the Lord is ultimately negative. You've taken care of the negatives. Now you can overflow because you have been filled with Him.

One of the surest ways to make "always abounding" a continual reality is to follow the simple formula written by Paul to the Christians at Philippi: "Rejoice in the Lord always; again I will say, Rejoice" (Phil. 4:4).

1. Paul told the Philippians, "I have learned, in whatever state I am, to be content. I know how to be abased, and I know how to abound; . . . I have learned the secret of facing plenty and hunger, abundance and want" (Phil. 4:11–12). What qualities of character did Paul reveal in these verses? What influence would such characteristics have on one's ability to "rejoice in the Lord greatly" (v. 10) or "rejoice in the Lord always" (v. 4)? Name any situations which you can recall from the apostle's life which put these concepts to a severe test. How did Paul's life show his ability to face all of life with joy? Did he discover ways to express joy even in the small things of life (Phil. 4:14–18)?

2. Paul's letters prove that negative things often happened to him. Do these usually intermingle with life's positives? What dominant attitude seemed to have been expressed by the apostle? Give any personal examples of the truth of Psalm 30:5. Have you ever experienced the reality of Psalm 126:5? Does this imply the possibility of a considerable time lapse between sowing and reaping? How should one act in the interval? Does Psalm 118:24 imply a fatalistic acceptance of everything that happens or a genuinely positive approach to each day's living? Discuss.

3. We are encouraged to abound—to have an overflowing spirit. What are some sources of such living? Discuss Romans 5:15 and I Corinthians 15:58. Name some practical ways in which one can "abound in the work of the Lord." How does one "abound in hope" (Rom. 15:13)?

4. How does the overflow of one's love (Phil. 1:9) produce an abundant life? What does Paul command the Corinthians to excel (abound) in (II Cor. 8:7)? Why did he emphasize it so strongly at the end of the verse? How would the phrase "that you may always have enough of everything and may provide in abundance for every good work" (II Cor. 9:8) enrich one's own life?

How does an outgoing, generous spirit produce inner joy? How did Paul associate joy and poverty (II Cor. 8:2)? Does there seem to be an incongruity in such thinking? Why, or why not?

5. What part does rejoicing have in an abounding life? In what practical ways does one rejoice (Isa. 35:2)? Distinguish between rejoicing with joy and rejoicing with singing. Have some Christians failed to practice rejoicing because they don't know how to sing? Should we so closely relate rejoicing with singing? Why, or why not? How does one "with joy . . . draw water from the walls of salvation" (Isa. 12:3)? How could the entire twelfth chapter of Isaiah be used as a pattern for one's own rejoicing? Discuss each concept presented in the chapter.

6. Discover some scriptural guidelines for rejoicing (Ps. 23:1; Ps. 119:14; Prov. 5:18; Prov. 24:17; Luke 1:47). What part can the actual words of Scripture play in one's rejoicing (Ps. 119:162)? Demonstrate how one might use poetic sections of the Bible, such as Psalm 121, as expressions of rejoicing. Suggest other portions of Scripture that are meaningful in praising the Lord. Read some of these portions aloud in a prayerful manner. In a group, one person could read expressively as the others bow in prayer.

7. Is there a manner in which one need not speak in order to rejoice (Ps. 16:11)? What could one do in God's presence? Are there ways in which meditation produces abounding joy (Ps. 51:8)? How does one "rejoice with joy unspeakable and full of glory" (I Peter 1:8, KJV)? How does one put his whole heart into rejoicing (Zeph. 3:14)? How can one make abounding joy an ever-present reality without being phony (Isa. 55:12)?

15
Becoming a Caring Person

The big print on a bumper sticker said, "Who cares? We do!" The smaller print listed an organization seeking to help crippled children. Such bumper stickers, and the people they represent, seem rare. The way most people drive—and often live—would most appropriately be epitomized by a bumper sticker which would say, "Every man for himself!"

Most people seem so involved in making a living, establishing a reputation, building their own household, or pursuing their own entertainments that they pay little attention to others. Only occasionally are they shocked by desperate needs around them. Then, their caring is done on a token, often one-time, basis.

If we say, "I don't care what you do," we usually mean we don't think it's our business to interfere in the lives of others. Unfortunately, we sometimes carry this attitude into too many human relationships, keeping aloof from the needs around us.

What a contrast to the Christ of the New Testament. He never separated Himself from caring. He'd even minister to those who'd brush against His garments in a crowd, hoping that the touch would bring help. He was the caring Christ.

1. Possibly the greatest characteristic we learn about Christ from the gospels was that He cared about the needs of people. What type of ministries always accompanied His preaching (Matt. 9:35)? What does the phrase, "when he saw the crowds, he had compassion on them" (Matt. 9:36), mean? Could we apply dictionary definitions of compassion to the ministry of Christ: suffering with another; fellow-feeling; sympathy; pity that inclines one to help another? How could Christ have such compassion on an entire crowd? Was this a common attitude of His (Matt. 14:14; Mark 6:34)? How did Jesus reveal His compassion in Matthew 15:32–36 and Mark 8:1–8?

2. How did Christ show compassion for individuals? How did He respond to the two blind men (Matt. 20:29–34)? Consider the story of a widow who was burying her only son (Luke 7:11–15). How did those attending the funeral react to Jesus' ministry? Are these incidents in line with Christ's announcement about Himself concerning ministering (Matt. 20:28)? What challenge did He give in verse 27? Was this a new concept to most of His hearers? Is there any significance in the fact a second gospel writer recorded this same conversation (Mark 10:43–45)?

3. Is a "compassionate God" an Old Testament concept? What pictures does the psalmist present in Psalms 111:4, 112:4 and 145:8? How have we experienced His being "full of compassion" (Ps. 145:8, KJV) or "abounding in steadfast love"? How do you picture a gracious God? What did Paul say that God told Moses (Rom. 9:15)? How did God express this to Israel?

4. How did the early followers of Christ grasp the meaning of the Lord's compassionate ministry? For what did Christ promise they would receive reward (Matt. 25:31–36)? What other evidences do we have that His followers knew the secret of ministry (Luke 8:1–3)?

5. Discuss some of Christ's concepts of ministry. How should we treat someone who asks us to give him something we possess (Matt. 5:42)? On what basis should we give to others (Matt. 10:8)? What did Jesus tell the rich young man he ought to develop as a philosophy (Matt. 19:16–22)? How would this fit into our culture? How did the young man's response reveal a lack of concern for others? What did his response reveal about his concerns and character?

6. When Jesus sent His disciples out to proclaim the kingdom, how were they to prepare (Luke 12:32–34)? What were they to do as they went out preaching (Matt. 10:7–8)? Does one ever get the impression that Jesus believed a caring ministry was more valuable than a preaching ministry? If not, how much emphasis, percentage-wise, do you think He placed on caring? Why is a caring ministry so vital to the validity of a preaching ministry, even today?

7. How did Jesus describe those who made a pretense at caring (John 10:12–13)? What condemnation did He heap upon Judas' sudden burst of pseudo-interest in the poor (John 12:1–8)? What do you think motivated Judas' proposition?

8. What did Paul say fulfilled "the law of Christ" (Gal. 6:2)? Would this be contradictory to 6:5? In what manner do the two ideas complement each other? What compliment did Paul give to the Christians at Philippi (Phil. 4:10)? What did this reveal about their Christian character? How did Paul instruct the Corinthians about conducting a caring ministry (II Cor. 8:8–15)? To whom did he refer them as a good example of this, and how were the Corinthians to react (II Cor. 8:1–7)?

9. List ways Paul suggested to the Romans how they could fulfill a caring ministry (Rom. 12:9–10, 13, 20–21). How does Romans 13:8 summarize the caring ministry? In what manner ought such a ministry be conducted (Rom. 12:8)?

16

Being Forgiven and Forgiving

"I can forgive, but I can't forget." You've heard people say this about others who have offended them. Unfortunately the offended person seems not only to remember all the details but also to relish telling others about what happened. Then comes the hollow-sounding statement about forgiving and forgetting.

We try to accept such attitudes as genuine, knowing our own propensity for similar attitudes. But we usually walk away from such conversations feeling the person wasn't being truthful, especially with himself, about being a forgiving person. Somehow we sense that forgetting, although it is difficult to do, is a necessary part of the forgiving process.

Is not this the manner in which God forgives? The psalmist poetically portrayed this, "As far as the east is from the west, so far does he remove our transgressions from us" (Ps. 103:12). He doesn't continually remind us or others that we have sinned. In fact, we, being justified by faith in the death of Jesus Christ, like to claim that we now stand before God just as if we had never sinned. That's genuine forgiveness. God blanks our sins out of the record book through the blood of Christ!

1. What does Jeremiah 31:34 teach about how God forgives? What does it mean when God says, "I will remember their sin no more"? Were there any conditions placed on this type of forgiveness by God? When was this promise to be fulfilled (see vv. 31–34)? How did Isaiah pray concerning God's remembering iniquity (Isa. 64:8–9)?

2. How thoroughly can one expect God to forgive (Ps. 25:18)? Does God forgive all our sins if we lump them together when we ask for forgiveness, or should we pray about each sin? Discuss. Does asking for forgiveness for specific sins show a greater desire to rid oneself of sin? What kind of attitude did forgiveness inspire in the psalmist (Ps. 103:1–5)?

3. Are there times when whole nations are guilty of sin? Give ancient and modern examples. Does God forgive an entire nation for its wrongdoings? What was God's plea in II Chronicles 7:14? How did Solomon pray concerning the entire nation of Israel (II Chron. 6:36–42)? How confident was Moses that God would forgive the entire nation of Israel for its sin (Exod. 32:30–35)?

4. What type of life does Paul describe as coming to the person who is forgiven (Rom. 4:7–8)? What does he mean by "the Lord will not reckon his sin" against him? How does forgiveness come to an individual (I John 1:9)? How does the life and death of Christ enter into the forgiving process (Eph. 1:7; Col. 1:14)? How do we associate forgiveness of sin with the reception of eternal life? What happens within the forgiven person?

5. In the Lord's Prayer are the words, "Forgive us our sins, for we ourselves forgive every one who is indebted to us" (Luke 11:4). Immediately after giving the disciples this prayer, Christ added, "For if you forgive men their trespasses, your heavenly Father also will forgive you" (Matt. 6:14). How does God's forgiveness of us inspire our forgiveness of others? Why is this true?

6. Why is it that when we forgive, we are forgiven (Luke 6:37)? If we are forgiven much, what will be our attitude toward the one who forgives us (Luke 7:41–42)?

7. What is the model for our forgiving others (Col. 3:13)? Is this partial or complete? Can we say, "I will forgive but I can't forget" if we follow this model of forgiveness? What is the pattern for forgiveness given by Paul in Ephesians 4:32? What attitude undergirds one's ability to forgive others?

8. If you know someone has a grudge against you, what should you do? What did Christ teach in Matthew 5:23–24? How was this expressed in Mark 11:25?

17
You Shall Be Free Indeed

People throughout the world have a longing to be free. Many willingly die in the pursuit of freedom. Some seek freedom, not knowing how to define it.

We speak about our great freedoms: the freedom of expression, religion, the press, domicile, pursuit of happiness. Too often we take these for granted. A visit to a controlled society quickly brings our freedoms into sharper focus.

The dictionary defines freedom as not being subject as a slave to a master; enjoying personal liberty and rights to action; being at liberty; being allowed to go anyplace; not being kept in confinement. Freedom includes the ideas of being unimpeded, unrestricted, unhampered.

Interestingly, not until all the outside-of-oneself meanings are listed is reference made to inner freedom: acting of one's own will or choice; not being determined from without; acting willingly and spontaneously; being frank and open, ingenuous, unreserved.

1. Romans 6:18 and 22 state we have "been set free from sin." How was this accomplished? What is the "law of sin and death" (Rom. 8:2) from which we are set free? How does faith in Christ affect our freedom? What significance do we find in Paul's immediate statement about being "slaves of righteousness"? What does this mean? How is it an expression of being free?

2. Jesus proclaimed, "If the Son makes you free, you will be free indeed" (John 8:36). How does this dovetail into Paul's teaching in Romans? To what was Christ responding when He made this statement? Were His listeners thinking about political freedom or personal freedom? Does Christ lead people into political freedom? If not, why is Christianity usually opposed by dictatorships? Why are many countries where Christianity is the dominant religion also democracies?

3. The New Testament was written in a master-slave culture. Why didn't the early church deal with the issue of slavery? How did Paul instruct slave Onesimus and slave owner Philemon (see the Book of Philemon)? In what way was Onesimus free? Was this satisfactory for a full-orbed life? What instructions did Paul give to slaves and slave owners in Ephesians 6:5–9? Why did it take the church so long to develop an abolition stance?

4. Paul instructed the Corinthians: "I want you to be free from anxieties" (I Cor. 7:32). What example of anxiety did he give? What is the best way to have freedom from anxiety? How can one arrive at the state of mind and heart advocated by Christ in Matthew 6:25, "Do not be anxious about your life, what you shall eat or what you shall drink, or about your body, what you shall put on"?

5. Note how Paul describes his freedom in I Corinthians 9:19. What conditions did he put on himself because he was free? Was this an honest expression of freedom? For what purpose did he thus act? Is it possible to be totally free in oneself and yet be subjected to others? How could this be true in today's world?

6. Jesus stated that discipleship to Himself first brings a person to the truth. He proclaimed Himself to be the source of truth: "I am the truth." He told His disciples, "You will know the truth, and the truth will make you free" (John 8:32). Why does truth, especially the truth about which Christ spoke, produce freedom? Describe the freedom you enjoy through knowing Jesus Christ. Does scientific truth have the same effects upon human personality? Why, or why not?

7. How is freedom being abused in our society? How can a Christian help to correct such situations? What help does Peter give (I Peter 2:16)? How free is a person in human society? What guiding principles must be followed? What can an individual do to insure greater freedom for everyone?

8. In what tangible ways does personal freedom motivate you to enhance the freedom of others? What are your present involvements in the promotion of freedom?

18
Gaining Those Gentle Attributes

Most of us long to possess the finer qualities of true Christian character, including these fruits of the Spirit—patience, kindness, gentleness, self-control, and the ability to be long-suffering. We somewhat reservedly admit to at least a desire to understand what it means to be meek. All these characteristics we know to have existed in Jesus Christ . . . and we desire to be like Him.

Patience is the ability to endure any situation with calmness and composure. It means to forbear (be tolerant) under provocation of any kind, or to calmly abide an issue until it is resolved.

Kindness means a person possesses the ability to be sympathetic, considerate, generous, and courteous—all with a calm spirit. It also involves having an exceptionally friendly disposition which considers the wishes and interests of others prior to one's own. Kindness means being loving, tender, and grateful.

Gentleness involves being noble, generous, and

courteous (especially being polite in dealings with others). A gentle person possesses calmness of spirit.

A person who has self-control is not easily angered. He is even-tempered and in control of his emotions when he is under pressure. Self-control means a person has a sense of direction and moral restraint in the presence of evil.

Long-suffering is the ability to endure . . . and keep on enduring regardless of the reactions of others or the changes in circumstances. It means a person is not anxious or ruffled by circumstances.

A meek person is free from self-will which pushes oneself above others. He is patient and unresentful, a person who, in Aristotle's definition, doesn't take the extreme course. Meekness means ruling one's emotions, not being ruled by them, and living in balance. A meek person is in control of his passions, willing to yield to the desires of others, considers others to be better than himself. He is willing to be led.

1. What did Jesus mean "In patience possess ye your souls" (Luke 21:19, KJV)? In what setting did He make this statement? How does one "possess [his] soul" by a facet of his character? In what ways can one draw upon the God of steadfastness (that is, patience; Rom. 15:5)? Wouldn't you think that suffering could produce the opposite of patience? Aren't we often frustrated because of our pains? How does Paul instruct the Romans (5:3–5)?

2. Why do we have such a great need for patience (Heb. 10:36)? Does it seem contradictory to "run *with patience* the race that is set before us" (Heb. 12:1–2, KJV; italics mine)? How is this done? Doesn't it usually take considerable tenseness or intensity to win a race? Isn't this opposite to the leisurely meaning we attach to patience? How does one "let steadfastness [patience] have its full effect" (James 1:3–4)? Is becoming patient something automatic, or must we work at it (II Peter 1:5–9)? (This is translated "steadfastness" in the RSV, "patience" in the KJV.) Does not James command us to be patient (James 5:7–8)? How will this help to "establish your hearts"? How are we to express this toward weaker believers (I Thess. 5:14–15)?

3. How does Nehemiah 9:17 picture the kindness of God? Does Psalm 54 intimate that God is kind? How? What does Joel 2:13 say characterizes God?

4. Paul's testimony to the Corinthians lists kindness equally with several other characteristics. List these and compare them to kindness (II Cor. 6:3–9). What is Paul's command to the Colossians (Col. 3:12–15)? How does he summarize all these good attributes (Col. 3:14)? To what does Peter say we ought to add kindness (II Peter 1:5–8)?

5. Carefully review the meaning of gentleness. Give examples from life. In what ways could Paul say "we were gentle among you" (I Thess. 2:7–8)? How did he instruct Timothy to act toward those he taught (II Tim. 2:24)? How would this be done in a teaching situation? By whom did Paul entreat the Corinthians to be gentle (II Cor. 10:1)? What authority does this add to gentleness? James says that the wise are gentle. How is this gentleness expressed (James 3:17–18)?

6. Discuss self-control as one of the fruits of the Spirit (Gal. 5:23–24). How does the Spirit make this a characteristic of the believer?

7. What does it mean to be long-suffering? How is God long-suffering toward us (II Peter 3:9)? How was this expressed early in the history of Israel (Exod. 34:6–7; Num. 14:18)? Is this expressed toward individuals also (Ps. 86:15–17)?

8. How does one express this attribute in dealing with others (Eph. 4:2)? What other attitudes does Paul suggest should accompany one's long-suffering (Col. 1:11)?

9. Do you want to be meek? Discuss what meekness means. Consider what scriptural references say about meekness (Pss. 22:25; 147:6; 149:4). How was Moses very meek (Num. 12:3)? How was Jesus "meek and lowly in heart" (Matt. 11:29)? Does this mean He didn't defend what He believed? What does it mean? How do you attain this attribute? Why is it true that the meek are blessed (Matt. 5:5)? How does Peter describe the beauty of meekness (I Peter 3:3–4)? Why must we "receive with meekness the implanted word" (James 1:21)? Why does meekness in showing one's work demonstrate wisdom (James 3:13, 17)?

19
Being Good and Godly

Many evangelical Christians seem to think that godliness and goodness are in apposition to each other. They confuse the concept of doing good works as a means of salvation with doing good works as a result of salvation.

Ephesians 2:8–10 clears up the problem: "We are

saved through faith . . . not because of works" (vv. 8–9). As such "we are his workmanship" but now have a distinct purpose. Because we are "created in Christ Jesus" that specific purpose has been spelled out: "for good works, which God prepared beforehand, that we should walk in them" (v. 10).

It couldn't be made much clearer: we are first made godly (created in newness of life by the power of Christ alone) that we might live good lives. To have the one without the other is a biblically spiritual impossibility. According to biblical teaching, a godly life produces good; conversely, a good life can only spring from a godly heart.

James makes this clear in his debate on faith and good works: "Show me your faith apart from your works," he challenges, "and I by my works will show you my faith. . . . For as the body apart from the spirit is dead, so faith apart from works is dead" (James 2:18, 26).

1. Let's concern ourselves first with what Scripture says about being and becoming godly. Discuss these meanings of godliness: observant of the laws of God; wise in divine things; religious and pious; transformed by the power of Jesus Christ; living a God-like life; spiritual. List additional meanings and make reference to all these meanings when discussing the following texts. Some texts present one concept, some another. Choose the concept that the group believes best fits the text.

2. Several texts describe the Christian as being sanctified—set apart as holy (or godly), made productive in holiness (that is, in the characteristics of Jesus Christ). How does Paul state this to the Corinthians (I Cor. 6:11)?

What meaning do you give to this text? How are sanctification and justification related? How thoroughly is one sanctified (I Thess. 5:23)? What does this do for the entire personality? How does Scripture enter the process (John 17:17)? What persons of the Trinity are involved in the sanctification of the believer (Rom. 15:16; I Cor. 1:2)? How?

3. Why does Paul say godliness is a "great mystery" (I Tim. 3:16)? What elements of this mystery are known to the believer? To whom is godliness the greatest mystery? Paul also instructs Timothy to "train yourself in godliness" (I Tim. 4:7). How? Why is "godliness of value in every way" (v. 8) compared with attending to the development of the physical body? How valuable is physical exercise? Does Paul say one ought not pay attention to the development of the body? Discuss.

4. What danger does Paul allude to in I Timothy 6:5? How would we relate this to many evangelically-oriented positive-thinking approaches which lead one to believe that if he is related to God he'll succeed financially? Does I Timothy 6:6 "pooh-pooh" this modern concept? Why must we be careful when relating financial gains to our relationship to God? Would this mean that the poor aren't properly related to the Lord? Can the poor be godly? Give examples. What does Paul say might happen to the godly person (II Tim. 3:12)?

5. Why does Paul give Timothy so many admonitions to follow after godliness (I Tim. 6:11)? Is this because godliness can't be gained on a corporate basis and must always pertain to individuals? Explain. Check the reference Peter makes to the godly life (II Peter 1:3, 6; 3:11).

6. For what purpose does Paul say God gave us the Scriptures (II Tim. 3:17)? Why do we so often quote this text and yet seem to miss this most important point? What use is a person who has been made godly or purified (II Tim. 2:21)? How does God make us "perfect in every good work" (Heb. 13:21, KJV)? How does Paul describe the people God has "[purified] for himself" (Titus 2:14)? For what purpose do they live (Titus 3:8)? What attitudes do they convey? What challenge does Paul give to Titus personally (Titus 2:7)? How would one apply this in his own life today?

7. Should one worry about being condemned for doing good works (III John 11)? How should we promote good works (Heb. 10:24)? Does the problem of being condemned for doing good works lie more with the condemning person than with the condemned? What if we fail to do good works (James 4:17)? Should we ignore those who condemn us for doing good?

8. What good works should your group of Christian believers do in your own community? How will these works demonstrate godliness? Should such acts be done without bannering the fact we are Christians? Discuss. Describe the benefits of being leaven in society.

20
Humility and How to Attain It

How can one obtain what he has such difficulty describing? That's the basic problem with humility. Most people think they can describe a humble person, but when they attempt to define humility, they portray a characteristic they'd personally never want to possess. Usually the descriptions depict a milquetoast, a spineless, self-degrading person who really doesn't know how to throw his shoulders back and face the world.

The Bible presents no such image. In the Bible, humility is extolled as an extremely desirable characteristic, though even in biblical times it seems not too many people possessed it. The biblical descriptions don't seem to jibe with modern American definitions. Let's look more closely at honest definitions and see how they fit the biblical pattern.

A humble person is not proud. He is modest, unpretentious, yielding, gentle, lowly, compliant, unassuming, soft, submissive, and defers to others.

Maybe it would be well to present some opposites of humility—things one really wouldn't openly claim as good personality characteristics: arrogance, contentiousness, haughtiness, presumptousness, pride, self-assertion, and vindictiveness.

In our search to have positive growth in Christian living, we reach out for true biblical humility—nothing counterfeit, nothing of which to be ashamed, nothing which calls attention to itself. For true humility portrays the character of our Lord Jesus Christ.

1. Discuss the meanings of humility. Are there any of these characteristics which we honestly wouldn't like to possess? How many do we find within ourselves? Which ones seem to need the most development? Why? Do we have the feeling we'd like to modify these characteristics a little to better fit into our present ways of thinking and acting? Why? How? Do we have an aversion to the opposites of humility? Why? Why are most of us cautious about being truly humble?

2. Is humility something to be actively pursued? If so, why do many people act as if it is a by-product of other Christian virtues? Are they afraid to admit to humility? Are there any dangers in thinking oneself to be humble? Discuss all these questions thoroughly.

3. The Bible often presents becoming humble as an activity to pursue. What does II Chronicles 7:14 say accompanies humility? How does one humble himself before he does the other things mentioned in the text? What was God's reaction to Israel's humbling of itself in II Chronicles 12:6–8? What about God's reaction to the king's humbling himself (12:11–12)? Does it seem these and other Israelite leaders humbled themselves because of defeat in battle (II Chron. 33:1–13)? What conditions does Isaiah 2:9–19 describe as a means of humbling men? Do they respond voluntarily? Is the time of defeat a legitimate time to be submissive to God? Why do we often wait for similar circumstances?

4. It might surprise us that the Bible commands humility. How did Paul instruct the Colossians (Col. 3:12)? What other characteristics accompanied lowliness? How many could be classified as humility? What part does the mind have in attaining of humility (Acts 20:19, KJV)?

5. Why would God offer a reward for humbling oneself (James 4:10; I Peter 5:6)? Should this be a prime motivation for becoming humble? Why, or why not? In what ways do you think God exalts the humble? Would the person be aware of such exaltation? Describe ways in which an individual becomes humble before God.

6. What picturesque language does I Peter 5:5 use in describing how one attains humility? According to the first part of this verse, what should govern the relationship between younger and older believers? How would a lack of submission indicate a lack of humility? Explain the phrase, "God . . . gives grace to the humble." What is this grace? What does it have to do with the development of Christian character? Could we associate this grace with graciousness? How?

7. Does one's concept of service and ministry depend on his attitude of humility concerning himself (Matt. 20:26–28; Mark 10:43–45)? How does the humble person exemplify the character of Christ? How does the use of one's gifts depend upon a humble attitude (I Peter 4:8–10)? How is this expressed in Romans 12:7?

21
Practicing Justice

Our pledge of allegiance to the flag ends with these dynamic words: "with liberty and justice for all." Yet we, like so many other nations around the world, still have many injustices. One of the most glaring is our belief that we have equal justice under the law. Yet those with money and power usually do not pay the same penalties for breaking the law as do the poor who break the same laws. In some areas of America, color of skin and one's national origin still determine job placement or advancements, even though the laws say we must practice no discrimination. Subtle discrimination, which is an injustice, can circumvent the laws.

Justice means equality of opportunity, equality of treatment under the law, impartiality toward all citizens, dealing with equity, uprightness, fairness, and integrity. It means freedom from prejudices or bias, not favoring one more than another.

Justice isn't simply obtained through or maintained by society on the basis of laws. It isn't totally the responsibility of our judicial or political system. Justice must be practiced by individuals as well. But it needs a motivation deeper than law. It needs to spring from people who are just. And what better wellspring than the heart of the Christian?

1. How does Psalm 89:14 describe the character of God? What does it mean that these attributes are "the foundation of thy throne"? How is this emphasized in Psalm 25:8–10? What message does Isaiah 45:20–23 communicate? From an understanding of the justice of God, what appeal does the psalmist make to God (Ps. 82:3–4)?

2. What was the promise made by God through Jeremiah 23:5–6? What would distinguish His reign as king? How is this amplified in Isaiah 11:1–5? Why were these prophecies so important at the time they were made? Give examples of how Christ "[executed] justice and righteousness in the land" during His earthly ministry. Are these prophecies still being fulfilled through Christ's followers? How? What futuristic elements do they contain?

3. How does Ecclesiastes 2:18–21 describe one of the inequities of life? How should one react in similar situations? Can we leave such situations to God and simply do what we sense is our portion of the responsibility?

Describe the attitude of the psalmist (Pss. 98:9; 99:4). What do we derive from his statement, "I walk in my integrity" (Ps. 26:1, 11)? How is this simplified in Proverbs 20:6–7?

4. Do we get a sense of well-planned action from Scripture passages which talk about justice? Discuss the following texts: "the path of the righteous is like the light of dawn" (Prov. 4:18); "the mouth of the righteous brings forth wisdom" (Prov. 10:31); "a righteous man . . . walks in his integrity" (Prov. 20:7). How is this applied on an extremely practical basis? (Discuss both Deuteronomy 25:15–16 and Proverbs 11:1.) Why was this so important in the Jewish culture? Why pick on such a seemingly small item in society? What defense did the poor have against being cheated even at this level?

5. Notice the distinction concerning justice and righteousness in Isaiah 56:1. Discuss both aspects. How is this amplified by Paul in I Timothy 1:8? Is emphasis again placed upon action? What does Paul mean by using the law lawfully? Is this simply to be a negative "I don't break the law" approach or should some positive action be made in applying the law we know? Discuss.

6. Justice should be shown in our one-to-one relationships. How was this to be expressed in a church fellowship (I Tim. 5:21)? To whom was Paul particularly addressing these remarks (I Tim. 5:17)? Is there danger for church leaders to become partial? What motivates partiality even in churches? How does James deal with the problem (James 2:1–7)? What corrective does James 2:8 offer? What does James say partiality really is (James 2:9–10)? Why such a severe condemnation?

7. What are some of the promises made to those who deal justly and walk uprightly? Would you like the benefits suggested in Psalm 84:11? Why? What does Proverbs 15:21 say the upright man possesses? How can this be applied in dealing justly?

8. What situations within your community or state need the attention of the principles of Christian justice? How can individuals first deal with known injustices and then apply correctives? Where does one start? How does one make sure he is applying Christian principles? Review some of these principles and list situations in which they can be applied.

22
Can You Love Too Much?

During the past decade, some psychologists have suggested one of the main causes of homosexuality is "too much loving" by a parent during child-rearing days. Unfortunately these psychologists seem to limit their concept of love. They concentrate on the areas of love dealing with erotic sensations and affections. Too much of these types of love, if demonstrated out of self-gratifying desires of the parent, will cause problems both in the manner in which the child reacts to others and in his understanding of love. But little evidence has been given to substantiate the claim that a person can truly love another too much. This of course means that the person knows and demonstrates the meaning of true love.

Let's go back to the ancient Greeks to discover the fullest meaning for love. The English word *love* is too inclusive. One can use it to mean sexual indulgence or the giving of one's life on a battlefield in support of his country. The Greeks used three words to particularize the meaning intended.

Eros refers to sexual love, sensual stimulation, or indulgence. It also refers to that warm emotional feeling one gets by contact with a member or members of the opposite sex. Erotic love is necessary for a good, enjoyable marriage relationship; it is perfectly legitimate in the marriage context. Governed by certain limitations, erotic love is also legitimate in all of society. It partially draws the sexes together at several levels of emotional contact. Eros stimulates boy-girl relationships. In the Christian context, these relationships have very definitely proscribed boundaries; eros is only allowed "all the way" in marriage.

Phileo refers to companionship—that which draws people together in friendship. Erotic sensations are not needed or desired. This sort of love is expressed in girl-girl and boy-boy relationships. Friends—those who enjoy each other's company, share like interests, and discuss problems exhibit this love. An excellent biblical example is David and Jonathan.

Agape refers to self-sacrificing or self-giving love. This love is not dependent upon the object being loved, but is freely expressed out of the heart of the giver. The desire of the lover is for the benefit of the loved. The benevolent thoughts or actions one has toward another are not for personal gain, but for the gain of the other. God so loved the world that He gave—agape love. Jesus loved (agape) us and gave Himself for us.

1. What type of love dominates present-day television programs and modern music? Why is there so much attention being paid to this type of love? Is it the easiest to express? Discuss. Why is erotic love often mistaken for the other types of love? Can erotic love be enduring? When? How? Would erotic love be enhanced by the expression of other types of love? How?

2. What should Christian parents teach their children about erotic love? How can this be done naturally? Should we favor sex-education classes in schools? Why, or why not? If we believe sex education should be taught in the home, how can it best be taught? Do parents need outside help? What is available? What are other Christian parents using?

3. What were the circumstances surrounding the platonic relationship that developed between David and Jonathan (I Sam. 17:48—18:1)? Describe the intensity of this relationship (I Sam. 18:1–5). What was Saul's first reaction to this relationship (v. 5)? What changed this relationship (I Sam. 18:6–9)? Describe some present-day attitudes which can ruin similar relationships. What was the basis for Saul's turnabout in attitude (18:12)? What was the secret of David's success (18:14)?

4. Describe the manner in which Jonathan expressed platonic love toward David (I Sam. 19:1–3). How did he defend David when speaking to Saul (19:4–5)? Was Jonathan persuasive (v. 6)? Look through chapters 19 and 20 for illustrations of how Jonathan cemented his friendship with David. What does this teach us about developing friendships today? What are the basic ingredients of a friendship? Are there degrees of friendship? How does one deepen friendship? What place does trust have in friendship?

5. In II Samuel 1:17–27 we read David's eulogy for Saul and Jonathan. How did David react to Jonathan's death? Is such a reaction natural? What further blessing came from this relationship concerning Jonathan's son (II Sam. 21:7–9)? How did David pay final respect to both Saul and Jonathan (II Sam. 21:12–14)?

6. Discuss verses which present agape love. Who demonstrates this type of love best (John 3:16–17)? How enduring was the love of Christ (John 13:1)? How extensive did Jesus say His love was toward the disciples (John 15:9)? How did the Father love the Son? To what extent did the Father demonstrate His love (I John 4:10)? Under what conditions does God love us (Rom. 5:8–11)?

7. How is agape love supposed to influence our reactions to one another (I John 4:7–12)? How does agape love originate (I John 4:19)? Why did Jesus call loving one another a new commandment (John 13:34)? Had He not taught that people should love each other? Didn't He state that the commandments could be summed up in two commands? What were these commands (Matt. 22:36–40)? Why did Jesus say that all the law and the prophetic teachings depended on these two commandments? Why do you think Jesus' hearers seemed to have missed the fact that love toward God and love toward neighbors were Old Testament teachings? Discuss Deuteronomy 6:4–7 and Leviticus 19:18.

8. What new concept is presented by the Lord in Matthew 5:44 and repeated in Luke 6:27? How is this possible? Can this be shown on any national scale? How? To whom?

9. What does Jesus mean "If you love Me, keep My commandments" (John 14:15, 21, 23)? What are these commandments, other than to love? Does this involve many practical fields of application? Name some. How do most of us score in this type of loving?

10. What does I Peter 1:22 tell about motives in loving? Is it possible to show agape love out of an impure motivation? How? What does John caution against (I John 3:18)? What does Paul mean in Romans 13:8–9? Is this possible in our society? Is there any danger in showing too much agape love? Explain.

23
Living a Peaceful Life

As one looks out over the world, peace seems a mockery. Some nations always seem to be clashing with their neighbors. Wars break out somewhere around the globe every few months. Old skirmishes continue. Some historians have calculated, from their studies of nations, that the world has known peace for less than two centuries in the millenniums of recorded history.

Somehow we've developed a warring mentality. Almost every American, including Christians who claim to know "the peace which passes all understanding," believe war is inevitable. Some Christians even take a fatalistic view, believing Christ prophesied the inevitability of continual war when He said, "You will hear of wars and rumors of wars" (Matt. 24:6). Since these Christians believe they have no power to reverse prophecy, why try to change the world? Why try to play the role of peacemaker?

Accompanying this interpretation has come a rather surprising philosophy. These Christians are not basically neutral toward war. They have strong ideas about national defense and the concept of participating in "just wars." While such Christians are quite vocal about their ideas of prophetic interpretations concerning the inevitability of military involvements, especially in confrontation with Communists, other Christians desire only to concentrate on personal peace. The Scriptures have much more to say about peace at this level. Even Jesus had more to say about peace on an individual basis.

Is it possible to reason from the basis of personal peace to community and national peace? What would you include in Jesus' statement, "Peace I leave with you; my peace I give to you; not as the world gives do I give to you. Let not your hearts be troubled, neither let them be afraid" (John 14:27).

1. Notice that peace was to be a national phenomenon (Lev. 26:6). What were the conditions which Israel had to meet (Lev. 26:1–13)? What else would accompany this peace? What threat hung over the people if they did not obey (Lev. 26:14–39)? How would the individual be affected in this situation? What benediction did the Lord pronounce in Numbers 6:26? Who were the beneficiaries? Does Psalm 29:11 have a nationalistic application? What?

2. What was God's promise to David concerning Solomon (I Chron. 22:6–9)? Why wasn't David a man of peace? What wouldn't God allow because of his warring nature and involvements? How could Solomon become a man of peace? What benediction did David give to his son (I Chron. 22:11–16)?

3. Why would some cry "Peace, peace" when there is no peace (Jer. 6:14; 8:11)? Do people ever get so desperate they will accept counterfeits of peace? Give examples from modern history. What needs to undergird true peace (Isa. 32:15–18)?

4. Isaiah 9:6–7 describes one who is the Prince of Peace. Was He to bring peace on a national basis? How? How did Christ ultimately produce peace (Col. 1:20)? What type of peace was this? Why is peace with God so important? Why was it so costly? Was this the peace which Paul declared in salutations to each church (e.g., Rom. 1:7; I Cor. 1:3; II Cor. 1:2)? Why do you think Paul always associated peace with grace? What does the peace of God do for individuals (Phil. 4:7; Col. 3:15)? Could it be applied on a group basis? Why, or why not?

5. Describe the peace listed as a fruit of the Spirit (Gal. 5:22). Is this the peace promised by Jesus in John 14:27? Why could Jesus call peace "my peace"? How did He contrast His peace with the peace the world gives (John 14:27; 16:33; 20:21)? Was this an admission that you can get peace in this world? Discuss. Contrast the quality of His peace with the world's peace.

6. Should we make peace an active pursuit or simply accept it as a part of our relationship to God (Ps. 34:14; Rom. 14:19)? Discuss. Does this mesh with the concept of Romans 8:6? What does it mean to be spiritually minded?

7. Why would Paul admonish Timothy to follow after peace (II Tim. 2:22)? How does the writer of Hebrews 12:14 state this concept? How does one do this on an active basis? What does Romans 2:10 say produces peace?

8. What effect does pursuing peace have on the pursuer (James 3:18)? What position should one try to maintain with others, according to Romans 12:18? What can one do when others don't want to live peaceably? How can one fulfill Matthew 5:9 in personal relationships? in community and national situations?

24
Understanding One's Gifts

Probably there's no other area of Christian doctrine in which there has been so much confusion as in the area of gifts. Possibly the main reason centers in a certain clamoring to possess a gift. Some people seem to present the idea that if you don't know what your gift is, you aren't spiritual. This is contrary to Scripture. One can never be proud of his gift. Gifts are given to be used humbly. In fact, this is one of the great problems Paul addresses in I Corinthians 12. The Corinthians were boasting about their spiritual gifts.

To look for a gift doesn't seem consistent with Scripture. Nor does parading one's gift. A casual perusal will reveal that some gifts are not definable. How does one specify the limits or characteristics for the gift of "helps" or the gift of "faith"?

A search of Scripture to better understand gifts should lead to humility, not to an attitude of "look at what the Spirit has given to me." Such an attitude, as is often expressed by some who claim the gift of speaking in tongues, can come only from a carnal heart and not from the gracious Holy Spirit.

Also, one discovers why gifts are given. This is of ultimate importance. The *why* is as important as the *what* and *how*. No gift is given to call attention to the one who has it!

1. Webster defines "gift" as "the transfer of an entity voluntarily and without any value consideration of the recipient; that which is voluntarily transferred to another without the expectation or receipt of an equivalent." Would these meanings in any way apply to God's giving gifts to believers? Does anyone ever legitimately ask for a gift? Discuss.

2. Why did Paul place such strong emphasis upon "same Spirit," "same Lord," "same God" (I Cor. 12:4–6)? Remember this was spoken to the same people who quibbled over which preacher to follow (I Cor. 3:1–9). Is there significance in the fact these Christians had problems with the meaning of gifts, and were the only ones called "men of the flesh" (3:1) by Paul? Discuss. What significance do we discover in Paul's reference to *Spirit, Lord, God*? Is this a reference to the Trinity being involved in the giving of gifts? Discuss differences or similarities in the phrases "varieties of gifts" (12:4), "varieties of service" (12:5), "varieties of working" (12:6).

3. Does I Corinthians 12:7 indicate any giving of gifts as a seal of approval upon one's life or beliefs? Is there any mention as to when the gift is given, especially in relation to faith in Christ as Savior? Why, according to Paul, are gifts given? Make sure this is discussed thoroughly and clear conclusions are made. Notice that we have no control over who receives a gift or when it is given (v. 11). What concept does Paul present when using the human body as an illustration of the church

(vv. 12–26)? Does this indicate unity in diversity? How? Is one part of the body more important than others? Is one part superior to others? Why would God give "the greater honor to the inferior part" (v. 24)? Is the answer in verse 25? How does this relate to gifts? Can one part of the body, or of the body of Christ, go off by itself or proclaim superiority to other parts? Is this being done in the body of Christ in our time? Why? How can it be corrected?

4. In Ephesians 4:12–13, Paul discusses further reasons for the giving of gifts. List these and discuss thoroughly. What are the results, according to verse 13? How are these ideas corroberated in Romans 12:4–13? If these are not produced, can we question the validity of the proclaimed gift or gifts? Why?

5. Make three lists of gifts: from Ephesians 4:11, from Romans 12:6–8, and from I Corinthians 12:8–10. Which of the gifts are repeated in all listings? Are these more important than the others in fulfilling the purposes stated in Ephesians 4:12–13? How do the three lists emphasize the gifts as means of edifying others rather than calling attention to themselves?

6. To what extent are believers supposed to express their gifts? What limitations are seemingly placed on each? Discuss each point made in Romans 12:6–8. How does each expression of a gift affect others? Does this call attention to the gift or simply show it in action? How precisely could one claim "I have the gift of . . ."?

7. What does Paul mean by "earnestly desire the higher gifts" (I Cor. 12:31)? Which of the gifts do you think he had in mind? Have we inverted the significance of gifts? Which ones seem to be the most important to Christians today? Why? Which are most sought after? Is this contrary to the teaching of Scripture? How can it be changed? How can we get back to a more biblical pattern?

8. After discussing the gifts of the Spirit, Paul makes a most significant and challenging statement at the end of I Corinthians 12:31. Why is the way of love more excellent than all the gifts? How can we follow it more realistically?

25
Have We Become More Like Jesus?

During the past twenty-four sessions we have studied various concepts leading to positive growth in Christian living. Our stated aims were to grasp more of what it means to be like Jesus Christ. We soon discovered we'd have to face some problems from the outside world, things that might hinder smooth progress. But most of our problems—and most of our development—comes via the inward look (who we are and who we desire to become).

Contrary to many who posit the idea that all one must do is take hold of the positives of life, we have discovered negatives must be dealt with. Then the positives can be readily sought and applied. There is no disgrace in recognizing negatives . . . or in dealing with them!

Now we come to an evaluation point. We want to look again not only at what we have studied, but also at what we have learned. Ideally the two are close together.

These sessions have been filled with penetrating questions. Our task is to discover whether the answers have also penetrated. It is only as our lives are invaded by God and the truths of the Scriptures that they are changed to more closely resemble the life of Jesus Christ. And no matter how much we think He possesses us, we'll always discover unconquered territory which He needs to enter.

In reviewing the various subjects today, may we again discover the joys of letting Jesus dominate our lives.

1. Why is it important that the Christian understand the problems around him, such as adversity, affliction, and persecution? What are the differences between adversity and affliction? What are some of the lessons one learns from afflictions? (Consult Psalms 94:12; 129:1–2; Isa. 48:9–11.) How does affliction develop character (Job 23:10; Prov. 17:3; Phil. 1:29–30)? How can we honestly say "Blessed are the persecuted"? If you are not being persecuted, what should your attitudes be?

2. What are some of the most bothersome inner problems each of us faces? How does the Christian deal with anger (Ps. 37:8; Eccles. 7:9; Eph. 4:26)? Why is it important to dispose of anger quickly? How can we keep from becoming angry? What does Scripture teach about anxiety? How does one cast all his anxieties upon God (I Peter 5:7)? How does bitterness affect one's spiritual development? What are some first steps in overcoming bitterness? How does one eliminate any "root of bitterness" (Heb. 12:14–15)?

3. Even with all our emphasis on the authority of the Bible, why is it possible to have doubts? How does one overcome doubts? How did Christ minister to doubters (Mark 9:23; Luke 18:27)? Discuss how to become a "believing Thomas" (John 20:25–29). Are doubts and fears related? How? What overcomes fears (II Tim. 1:7; I John 4:18)?

4. Looking at the positives, how can one always abound (Phil. 4:4, 10–12)? What are some sources of successful living (Rom. 5:15; I Cor. 15:58)? How does an outgoing, generous spirit produce inner joy? How deeply can we draw from our knowledge and experience to produce joy (Isa. 12:3)? How does one "rejoice with joy unspeakable and full of glory" (I Peter 1:8)?

5. How does my concern for others develop Christlikeness in me? What type of character is often portrayed in the gospel presentations of Christ (Matt. 9:36; 15:32–36; Mark 8:1–8)? Why is it more important to minister than be ministered unto? Does this develop Christ-likeness? How? Is forgiveness involved? How? How are we to be forgiving (Matt. 6:14)? What is the model for our forgiving others (Col. 3:13)?

6. In chapter 18 we discussed how to gain "those gentle attributes." Name some. How are they related to becoming more like the Master? How does one become patient? kind? gentle? What does it mean to be longsuffering? Is goodness something to be sought? How does it go hand-in-hand with godliness (Eph. 2:10)? How does one become "perfect in every good work" (Heb. 13:21)?

7. Why is justice toward others a good mark of a change to the Christian lifestyle? What does Micah 6:8 list as ways to please God? Does this mean that pleasing God involves considerable social involvement? Give examples from the life of Jesus.

8. What place must love have in all Christian living? What is agape love? How does it influence the effectiveness of our outreach? How does it show we've been transformed by Christ?

9. What aspects of these studies have been the most meaningful to you? What influenced you most to fuller surrender to Jesus Christ? What personal development of Christian character have you noticed in yourself?